NO M
PAIN

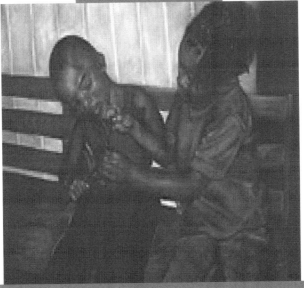

TRUTH ABOUT CHILDREN WHO GREW UP IN ABUSIVE FAMILIES

David A. Hatch, Ph.D.

CONTENTS

I Will Always Be reminded Of My Daughter's Death Through Her Children

I Was Four Years Old When My Mother Was Killed

Hurting Inside

Who Cares About My Pain?

3. Wounded Hearts

Thirty Seven And Wiser

A Story Of Hidden Pain

I Am An Hurting Black Male

4. The Solution

Trust in the Lord with all thine heart;

And lean not to thine own understanding.

In all thy ways acknowledge Him

And He shall direct your paths.

Proverbs 3:5,6

This book is dedicated to families who have hidden or inner hurts.

Special dedication and thanks to my God Mother, Mother Leola Martin, my wife, Lillie R. Hatch, my children Amber, Zaneta, Feranei and Larry who are my inspiration for this book:

ACKNOWLEDGEMENTS

Writing this book was a special experience. It brought back many memories and confirmed the need for a book like this. The many wounded and hurting people I have encountered are the central focus for creating this work.

Relationships individuals and families going through inner hurt have been invaluable. Their interactions and stories have given me exceptional insight into the world of many people who cannot express their hurts.

While writing this book, I was fortunate to have the help and support of some outstanding people, my wife, Lillie R. Hatch, gave me the will to complete this book by standing by my side, encouraging and assuring me that I could do anything I felt this strongly about.

I am deeply indebted to Mrs. Rita Hatfield for editing this book. My thanks to Mr. Curtis E. James for allowing me to use his original artwork, "Mending Hearts" on the front cover.

Dr. David A. Hatch

INTRODUCTION

Hurt is a powerful, degrading, humiliating form of abuse, especially when the people we love and trust the most cause the hurt. We have covered our hurt since the fall of Adam and Eve. God created man to live inside the Garden of Eden eternally in perfect harmony, without hurt or pain. However, hurt has existed from the moment Adam took the fork in the road and was kicked out of the Garden of Eden.

The result of inner hurt is a devastating form of abuse because others cannot see it, unlike how we can see a bruised cheek. Nevertheless, abuse affects us spiritually, mentally, and physically. Eventually, it destroys us if it is not stopped. It can bring physical, everlasting pain to the body in the form of diabetes, high blood pressure, kidney problems, AIDS, and other diseases.

God's grace allowed me to write *No More Pain* based on my personal experiences and others, and to produce the play *The Will To Survive: I've Got It,* a gospel musical drama based on the book.

My hope is to help someone identify and expose abuse; to provide solutions to heal that are inside; to bring the hurts outside and heal the body inside.

This book is for anyone who has ever been hurt by a personal, professional, or passing acquaintance, or a stranger. Unfortunately people who cause us the most hurt are usually the ones we love and are closes to, people we live with, eat dinner with and go shopping with, go to church with, and marry, our most intimate family and friends.

Child abusers risk going to jail just to satisfy their abnormal desires. Husbands batter their wives and after each beating promise never to do it again. The cycle of abuse must end. There is no color barrier or age limit for people who abuse other people.

You will read some testimonies of how people cover up their hurts: laughing on the outside while hurting on the inside; practicing homosexuality, pretending to be church-going Christians; husband abusing their wives and children; women abusing their children; relatives and friends sexually abusing young people; women prostituting, using drugs such as marijuana, crack, cocaine, and heroin. You will also read how they are healing their hurts. Scriptures are included to show you what God has to say about people hurting other people.

My hope is that by reading this book, you will tell someone about your inner hurt. If you know someone who is abused, share this book with that person. I hope that you will then have the courage to allow God to help you, as he helped me, to begin the healing process. Remember, God cares about you, and so do I.

Do you care about you?

SHARE YOUR THOUGHTS

I would love to hear your reactions to the stories in this book. Please let me know how they affected you. I also invite you to send me stories you would like to see published in future editions of *No More Pain.*

Send submissions to:
David A. Hatch, Ph.D.
TSO Network, Inc.
www.teensspeakingout.org
2711 Astoria Drive
Albany, Georgia 31701
229-449-9455
darchiehatch@gmail.com

I hope this book helps you in a way you did not think possible. God bless you and your entire family.

CHAPTER 1 HURTS

Of all the traps and pitfalls in life, self-disesteem is the deadliest and hardest to overcome, for it is a pit designed and dug by our own hands, summed up in the phrase. "It's no use- I can't do it"
Maxwell Maltz

Childhood into Adulthood

Childhood hurts, if not healed, become adult hurts. Webster's dictionary defines hurt as "to cause physical pain or injury to." You can see physical signs of hurt, such as red marks, bite marks, or bruises. Since the effects of these physical hurts are obvious, they are easily treatable. But what happens when you can't see the hurts?

Hidden hurts become inner hurts. They eat away at you and cause mental pain. For instance, children are easily hurt when others constantly tease them. Not only do their peers tease them, but also their parents and other caregivers tease them about their weight, height, or even about having freckles. When parents constantly reprimand children about low grades, or when there is no adult guidance provided, children can develop feelings of unworthiness and negative behaviors, and become overly aggressive. They can withdraw and become passive, thus allowing the pain to fester inside and develop into inner hurt.

These hurts harm our children emotionally because children's minds and spirits are more fragile than their bodies. By keeping these feelings inside, the hurts can delay physical growth. This inner hurt does not disappear. It is devastating because hiding hurt feelings is easy. The hurt remains inside and becomes part of the child's self-picture, which is carried through childhood into adulthood.

Obviously, physical abuse is painful. However, words can hurt even more than a slap in the face. Peers, and more importantly parents and caregivers, must be more aware of their own behavior toward children. When they feel belittled, children bury their feelings inside which often causes problems into adulthood.

Abusive Partners

Rate your experience with abuse. If you answer "yes" to any of the questions below, you are probably a victim of abuse.

Does your partner:
- Prevent you from seeing your family members
- Prevent you from seeing your friends
- Criticize your accomplishments
- Bully you
- Threaten you
- Hit you
- Punch you
- Slap you
- Beat you
- Kick you
- Threaten you with a firearm
- Prevent you from leaving your home
- Prevent you from getting a job
- Prevent you from continuing your education
- Forces you to have sexual relations
- Force you to engage in uncomfortable sexual acts that make you feel uncomfortable

As you can see, abuse does not always have to be a slap or a kick. Abuse is also words that adversely affect your daily normal actions. The most difficult step to take is to admit that you are being abused. When you can admit to the abuse, you have taken a necessary and important step to find your way out of the abusive relationship and to begin the healing process.

Look at the list again and make a decision to stop the abuse.

Physical and Behavioral Signs of Abused Children

Listed below are physical signs of abused children. Please remember, however, that *there are no set rules in stone* when dealing with sexually abused children. Some or none of these signs may be present to indicate child abuse.

Physical Signs
Venereal disease
behavior
Pregnancy
Bruised genitals
behavior
Recurring urinary tract infection
Difficulty walking
Difficulty sitting
Bloody underclothing
Change in eating habits

Behavioral Signs
inappropriate sexual

Extremes of behavior
Self-destructive

Sleep disorders
Nightmares
Eating disorders
Withdrawal
Fear of certain people
Fear of certain places
Starting fires
Uneasiness, anxiety
Low self-esteem
Suicide attempts

Statistics show that 88% of the times, children who are sexually abused are abused by family members. This tells us how imperative it is for us to watch for changes in our children's everyday patterns. Watch for changes in their normal, physical, and behavioral manners.

CHAPTER 2

TESTIMONIES

If you want to lift yourself up, lift someone else
BOOKER T. WASHINGTON

I have met many people who have experienced abuse in childhood or in adulthood. Some of the abuse was self-inflicted, and some of the abuse was caused by other people.

The following testimonies are from people who have experienced sexual, physical, and emotional abuse. Their stories go much further than the scope of this book. Observe what they are doing to heal their inner hurts.

Any names used are fictional, but the stories are real.

The following testimonies were written exactly the way they were spoken. Please be advised that some of the language and descriptions are extremely graphic. The words of the people who spoke to me about their lives have not been changed or altered. These are the true stories of events that have taken place in their lives. They are not pretty stories and some do not have a happy ending. There are many of you who have experienced and are still experiencing the same types of abuse spoken of in this book. Please know that you are not alone and there is hope. Your life can change and you can heal. I know it is possible because I have known abuse in my own life and I have also known healing. My hope is that for those of you who have lived through the nightmare of abuse and can relate to the raw truth spoken in this book, you will know beyond a shadow of a doubt that your life is valuable and you are loved. My hope is for you to become free from the prison of anger and mistrust. Even though you may not understand how this possible, please know that it is. God created you and believes your life is so valuable that he gave His own son to die for you. Jesus Christ willingly suffered horrible abuse and was crucified on a cross. He was not killed, but he chose to give his life for you and me. Jesus has the power to lay down his life and to take it up again. We possess the same kind of power. We can overcome anything just like He does.

If you have been going to church and listening to sermon after sermon and you still are struggling with your past or even your present, you are in for a pleasant surprise when you read what this book has to offer. You may have heard these kinds of things before, you can overcome, you can do all things through Christ who strengthens you, anything is possible if you only believe, faith heals, etc. All these things are true but you will find in this book exactly what these sayings really mean and how to apply them to your daily life. After all, what good does it do you to hear sermons week after week and nothing ever changes in your life, or if you try to read the Bible and do not understand it or if you have only a shallow understanding and your life is not affected very much? What you want is an end to your pain and suffering. You want to be happy. You want a solution, something that really works. You can have all that and more. You can do nothing to change your past, but you can do everything to shape your future. Get ready for a new life because it's yours!

I'M HURTING, BUT WHO NOTICES?

I was "daddy's girl," and I adored him. I know I could always feel safe with my daddy. It made me feel so good when he would call me his "little girl". We had wonderful talks and no one could have treated me more special.

So when my mother divorced him when I was four years old, I was devastated. Spending time with my daddy was now only on weekends. "You are the prettiest girl in your school and I bet you have lots of boyfriends," my daddy used to tell me. That made me feels very special because my daddy said it. Even at the age of four, having my daddy's approval was important to me.

I loved snuggling with my dad in the bed when I visited him on the weekends. One night when I slipped out of my room to sleep in my dad's bed, something weird happened to me that I could not understand. I felt my dad touching my private area. I was five years old.

By the time I turned seven, my daddy had penetrated my private area with his finger. The first time he tried to penetrate me with his penis, he couldn't. By the time I was nine years old, my daddy made me feel like I was the woman in his life. I began having sexual feelings for him and he would kiss me the way he used to kiss my mother.

I knew something was wrong with the way my daddy touched me. Looking back, I always wanted my daddy's approval and he made me feel special with what he was doing to me. He made it seem right. Even on weekends when my brothers spent the night, my daddy always treated us good. We would all have popcorn and watch movies together.

After I graduated from the sixth grade, my daddy promised to take my brothers and me to Six Flags over Georgia. However, when that day came, I felt something was wrong because my daddy had been drinking a lot. He kept going to the bathroom, and one time he stayed in there a long time. I thought to myself, "I hope he doesn't mess up this special time for me." You see, he had not touched me for a long time and I hoped it would stay that way. My dad shattered my hopes when he came out of the bathroom and headed straight for me. My brothers were sleeping right there in the living room, so I inched closer to them hoping my daddy would not touch me, but that did not stop him.

He put his hand on my head and began rubbing it. Before I knew what was happening, my daddy was penetrating my vagina with his index finger and thumb until he cut me with his fingernails. My brothers were there and I felt embarrassed, angry, and scared all at once. When my dad cut me with his fingernails, he went to the bathroom and washed his hands. For the first time, my dad made me feel dirty. I had never felt so inadequate with my dad. He belittled me, his "baby girl," and I hated him for that. I cried very hard.

I had to get even with him. While he was in the bathroom washing his hands, I called 9-1-1. I told the lady police officer my father had hurt me. I felt guilty and scared about reporting my dad. You see, I had reported him before but when the police officers arrived to arrest him, I lied to keep him from going to jail. So when I called this time, I thought the officers would not believe me. I was determined to make them believe me this time. I believed it was my fault, what my dad had been doing to me all these years, until the moment he washed his hands after penetrating me, making me feel dirty. My daddy had hurt me. I was only a child, his child.

As I grew older, my past sexual behavior haunted me. I continued being sexually active with boys much older than I. My behavior became self-destructive. I was obsessed with men and I would do anything to receive their attention. I would buy those gifts thinking this would make them happy. I would buy those clothes, shoes, jewelry, and gold. I would write them love poems and dedicated songs to them on the radio. I would buy those flowers and balloons. I would do anything to get their attention.

I even went as far as to do sexual acts I did not feel comfortable doing. My friends knew that if they made me feel guilty about something, I would eventually do it. So when one of my boyfriends pressured me in to having anal sex, I gave in.

One day my boyfriend drove me to an isolated area where he knew we would not be seen. What happened next was any girl's worst nightmare. He forced me to have anal sex; it tore my insides. My whole body felt sick. My breasts ached and my arms throbbed where he held them down. He thought he could ease my pain by kissing me passionately. I felt nauseous. Nothing could ease my pain.

It reminded me of the day my dad made me feel dirty by washing his hands after penetrating my vagina with his fingers. This time, I could not cry. I felt like a fool. When my boyfriend took me home, I foolishly roamed the cold, snowy streets for hours and became frostbitten. I was numb and felt my life was not worth living. I was determined to destroy myself. I tried to commit suicide by taking an overdose of pills. I blamed God for not protecting me.

To make matters worse, I married and had his child. I spent seven more years in this relationship. By the grace of God, I finally left him and I am beginning to build a life that will make my child proud. Through God's help, I know I can do good things for my child and myself.

I NEVER HAD THE LOVE OF A MOTHER

I was introduced to drugs at the age of 15, when I used Marijuana. It was introduced to me by kids I hung around in the neighborhood. At that time, I was drinking liquor — Wild Turkey 101. A grown man got me drunk and raped me. Before that, I was molested at the age of 9. The first time I was molested, it was done by my stepfather's brother. He was 16 years old, and I was 9. The second molestation was done by my stepdad who was 28, and I was only 15.

Marijuana was my drug of choice, off and on for years. My reason for using drugs was to take away the pain of the past sexual abuse. I stopped numerous times, but that didn't work. Drug abuse in the past has caused me to temporarily lose my kids to the state and experience extreme weight loss. What keeps me from constantly using drugs is reading the Daily Word. I'm working on changing my thoughts concerning drugs.

Feeling alone, rejected, and unloved caused me to use drugs at such a young age. I did not have anyone to emotionally support me. When I was a small child, I use to run behind my mother's car wanting her attention and love, but she always denied me. One day, my mom went to Burger King where she met my father who didn't live with us. She got in his truck, left me in her car, and had sex with him for money, and she didn't want to buy me anything.

My desire in life is to wipe away all my past pain and hurt. I want to rid myself and my life of all drugs and be the person God desires me to be. Basically, I want to be loved.

I WAS 16 WHEN I LOST MY VIRGINITY TO MY FATHER

I am the oldest of five girls. My mother and father married when she was only 17 years old. My parents provided us with anything we wanted. However, I started using drugs and alcohol at the age of 16. I enjoyed smoking weed and drinking. Therefore I used for a long time.

I lost my virginity against my will at the age of 16. My father took my virginity by molesting me, and that's when my life fell apart. I loved my father before then. I hate the ground he walks on now. I gave birth to my first child at the age of 17. However, I continued to drink, use drugs and hang out in the clubs and with the wrong crowd.

I missed being a child because I got pregnant, and by the time I turned 19 years old, I had two children. I was a single mother with two children, on welfare, and still drinking and smoking weed. I moved out of my mother's home and secured an apartment for my kids and me. Living on my own had some disadvantages; however, I loved being on my own. I thought I was doing something until I met this guy, Mark.

I loved this man more than life itself and I was head over heels in love. My smoking weed and drinking continued during this relationship. There seemed to be a dark side to this man. I later found out he was snorting cocaine. I was unaware for a long time. People were telling me he snorted cocaine but I did not believe them. I confronted him and he denied it. Throughout the relationship, I suffered; the lies, beatings, rape, stealing, and jealousy. I gave birth to two more babies at the age of 21. One day I got curious about cocaine, so I tried snorting. At first, I liked it and it was like "What's Happening" or "What's Going On." I had three more babies and they all had cocaine in their system.

My addiction progressed. I had three more babies and they all had cocaine in their system. By age 23, I had seven children. Being molested by my father followed me and nothing else mattered; however, I loved my children. One day DFACS visited my home and took four of my children. I just wanted to die. My kids meant everything to me.

I snorted cocaine non-stop. There was no limit to how high I got. Nights turned into days. I would go on a binge for three to four days non-stop because nothing else mattered.

By the time my other kids' father heard about my addiction, he took them from me. After that, I felt alone and afraid, but I continued to use drugs.

My addiction progressed. By the time I was 31 years old; I had birthed 10 children and had custody of none. I decided to check myself into a treatment center. It was a big change for me. I got myself a job and things started to get better. By the time I finished my treatment, I was discharged with a job and my own apartment.

LARRY'S TESTIMONY

My name is Larry. I am a grateful recovering addict. First of all, I would like to give all praises to God for allowing me, in spite of all of my shortcomings, to give my testimony.

I know of no other way to tell of this journey but from the beginning. I was born in Macon, Georgia into a very dysfunctional family. My mother and father often had disagreements. They argued, fought, and tore the whole house up.

Being born into this environment, the first emotion I felt was fear. I didn't know what love was and at that time I didn't know anything about God. My parents were God to me. I was afraid of them, afraid of what they might do to each other, and what they might do to me.

One day that fear came to life. My mother killed my father while he slept off a drunk. She poured gasoline on him and set him on fire. The house burned to the ground. One parent was dead and the other on her way to prison. That was my introduction to the experience of being homeless. I would encounter this experience often in my life.

My childhood had been stolen from me and now survival was the name of the game. I survived the stigma of growing up with people knowing that my mother was doing hard time. I survived by suppressing other little family secrets. I believed no one else had the right to know about them.

Years later my mother was released from prison, but she wasn't the same as when she went in. She had been affected mentally and physically. She came back hard and crude, and with that came mental and physical anger towards me. I didn't know if she really hated me, but at that time I knew I hated her.

After I came of age, I joined the Army. There was a war going on in Vietnam. I was more afraid of my mother than anything that was happening in Vietnam, I didn't know what the future held for me but I knew it had to be better than my past.

I was almost 23 years old before I saw my mother again. I was free and that was all that mattered to me at that time. I was free to make my own decisions about my life. Some of them were good and some weren't

I made the decision that whatever life threw at me, I would never hit a woman. My father made that mistake and I saw what happened to him; that was not going to happen to me. I also made the decision to drink and to do drugs. So far, that is the worst decision I have made in my life.

I thought my life as a child had been cursed, but that was nothing compared to my addiction to drugs. The saying in Vietnam was, "If you had to die, you might as well be high." The only problem was I didn't die. I came through the whole thing without a scratch, but I kept getting high. You name it and I did it — marijuana, morphine, heroin, liquor, beer, and LSD. Every day I was preoccupied with getting high. The drugs filled a void in my life and I thought I was really having fun. I had a lot of catching up to do but there was a price to be paid.

In Alcoholics Anonymous and Narcotics Anonymous we describe "insanity" as doing something over and over again, expecting to get a different result, and not getting it. Believe me, I was insane. In my addiction I couldn't do what I needed to do. Don't get me wrong, I really wanted to pay rent, bills, child support, and buy groceries, but those things meant nothing to me when I was drinking and doing drugs. I was addicted not only to drugs, but also to the lifestyle. The strip places and crack houses became my home.

In the past 30 years of active addiction, I have spent hundreds of thousands of dollars on drugs and an addict's lifestyle, while remaining homeless most of the time. One day I attended a church service. I heard something and I don't know if anyone else heard it. I believed it was Jesus, and what I heard changed my life.

I always believed in God, but every time someone talked about God, I found myself talking about what I didn't believe about God. I don't know why I did that but that's just the way it was. During my addiction, I read my Bible and prayed. I always kept that hope alive that maybe God still loved me and would someday grant me salvation. I needed saving and there was no denying that. I found out that the thing I needed saving from was myself.

I made a decision to enroll in a drug treatment center and started cleaning up my mind and my body. I started learning about addiction and myself. But, most of all, I started learning more about God. I learned about the plan He has for me and I began to realize that the drugs were separating me from that spiritual connection that we all must have with God, if we have any hope of living a clean and prosperous life.

MY ANGER COMES OUT

For 23 years I have held in my feelings toward people. I feel like I can't get close or trust anyone. This is because I have such deep hatred for people. I even hate myself. I don't know why. I've been taken advantage of, and raped at the age of 11. I feel so disgusted. I am so mad right now I could punch a hole in the freaking wall. I want to cry but my anger won't let me. Sometimes I wonder why I am still living.

I sometimes find myself taking it out on the one person I know loves me — my daughter. I never knew my mother or father. My aunt and uncle raised me. I was mistreated emotionally, verbally, mentally, and physically. There are a lot of things that need to come out before I end up hurting my daughter or myself.

All my life I have been called stupid and dumb. That made me feels so low. I have no self-confidence or self-esteem. I never had anyone to stand up for me. I don't get along with any of my family. They all treat me like I am nothing. It is sad because my daughter can't go home to see her cousins or just to be with any of our family. I am the only one she knows.

My daughter and I have been in and out of shelters, struggling since we have been in Georgia. I know that I won't be right with God until I can forgive my family and husband for what they have done to me, but it is hard to let go of the grudges. My hate is so deep that I don't think it can be cured.

I have been hurt so many times, and it has ruined my ability to trust. I don't trust people and won't let anyone get close to me without me thinking they want something in return. Sometimes, when I need help I won't ask for it. I would do without first. I used to ask for help in Alabama. People, men, or women would have helped me only if I would give them sex. But I never stooped to that level.

There are times when I have thought about killing myself or someone else. The devil is always putting thoughts in my head. Sometimes I wish I were dead. At 23 I tried to commit suicide. I took a bunch of pills and passed out at work. I woke up in the hospital with a tube down my nose. If I did not have Caitlin, I would be dead. The thought crosses my mind seven days a week. I still pray and that makes me feel better. But Satan never takes a day off. He is constantly in my head. And I can hear him saying, "Do it, Missy. Do it." Even when I look back on how miserable my life was, I do consider it.

When I was 15 I got pregnant. When my aunt told my uncle, he went off. When he came home to visit he would never let me hear the end of it. He would get drunk and call me "bitch" and "whore." He went around the neighborhood telling people I didn't know who my baby's daddy was, and that I had fucked everyone there. He made me look so bad to people. He even went as far as telling people that he had sex with me. What made it worse was that my aunt believed it. She asked me if it was true and I said "hell no." she didn't believe me.

I was only 17 and had to move out. I got my own apartment and put it in my aunt's name. I was still in high school but I made it. Once I moved out, I did not look back. My aunt and uncle don't know if I am dead or alive. I don't know if they are dead or alive. If I had only stood up to them I would not have all this anger and hatred. I never had a good relationship with either of them. I could never tell them my feelings or my thoughts without being cursed out. To this day, they don't even know that I was raped. I still carry that burden with me every day. That is why I am so protective of Caitlin. God got her in my life for a reason because she isn't supposed to be here.

Now that I have gotten my feelings out, I can start to let go of some of the anger and hatred that I have. God had already started the healing process in me. I will continue to pray every night until I am completely healed. It is going to take a lot of time, but God forgives us for what we don't forgive ourselves for. Why should I hate people for what they do to me? I hope that my story can help the next person who has been in the same situation. I found out that the longer I held it in, the more I plotted to kill someone.

I still have that urge at times. It is not as bad as it used to be, but I know as long as I hold this in, I will hurt someone. Now that it is on paper I can finally try to find closure.

I'm Running and I Can't Stop
God isn't alarmed when we hit rock bottom. He made the rock.
-Baptist Minister

Kathy told me about her life while she was in Atlanta's Metro Transitional Center. She was sent there after she was arrested for drug trafficking. How could a woman like Kathy be jailed for transporting drugs? When she was a little girl she had everything going for her. Kathy was reared by parents who provided for all her needs. Her family did not have much money, but her mother stayed at home with the children while her dad went to work. They lived in a housing project, but that didn't stop Kathy from believing her family was an all American family. So what went wrong?

The first sign of trouble was when Kathy was in the third grade. One day Kathy's mother sent her and her sister to the store. Kathy decided she wanted some cookies and cakes. Since her parents did not allow many sweets in the house, Kathy thought she could get away with stealing some from the store to keep for herself. However, Kathy was not aware that the store manager was watching her. As she was leaving the store with her stolen sweets, the manager confronted Kathy, and he sent her sister to get their mother before he called the police.

Kathy cried hysterically. She was frightened and begged the manager not to call her mother, but just let her go. She knew what the consequences would be when her parents found out about it. She would get a beating. The more she thought about what her parents would do, the more scared she became. Kathy broke away from the manager and blindly ran down one street after another until she was lost. By nighttime, she found herself in a stranger's garage. Hungry and tired, Kathy wished she were home no matter what she had to face. But she fell asleep and was later awakened by the police officer who notified her parents of her whereabouts. This was the first time Kathy had run away.

When her parents picked her up, Kathy could tell they had been very worried about her. "They were so glad to get me back they didn't even punish me for stealing," Kathy said. She could see and feel how much her parents loved her. From then on, Kathy developed a pattern of running away when she got into trouble. "Anytime something went wrong, I'd run." If her teacher sent a note home from school, Kathy would run away. If her parents argued, she would run away. If she fought with her sister, Kathy would run away. Kathy said she has never felt the love she experienced from her parents like the first time she ran away.

However, Kathy's parents grew tired of her running away. They gave her an ultimatum. They said, "If you don't like the way things are, too bad. It's our way or the highway." So by the time she was a teenager, Kathy said the streets were her home.

By age 17, Kathy had dropped out of school and she was pregnant. Her daughter, Jamie was born July 15, 1978. Kathy finally began to believe she had someone who would love her unconditionally. This belief was short-lived when Kathy's mother and sister felt the need to take care of Jamie because they believed Kathy was making self-destructive decisions. When the pressure of taking care of her daughter became too much, Kathy decided to join the army and she left Jamie in her mother's care.

When she joined the Army, Kathy began to feel some self-worth. "I met many people from all over the country," she said. "I always sent money home for my mother to take care of Jamie and to save for me." Kathy served for years in the army and received an honorable discharge. "My mother spent the money I sent home for her to save for me. The only thing she said was she had to take care of my daughter."

Kathy had no money to get her own apartment, so she had to move back with her parents in the housing project. Jamie did not have a job. She knew she had to take care of Jamie and she felt obligated to pay for living with her parents. She noticed how the dope boys and number runners would make lots of money fast. "I got involved with both. I liked the lifestyle they lived and wanted it for myself."

I had used drugs before this, but now I went all out. I used cocaine, marijuana, and I smoked crack. To support my drug habit, I stole $4600 cash from a numbers runner with whom I was dealing." Kathy was forced to leave New York and fled to Florida. She continued to sell drugs and run numbers. Kathy was also forced to leave Florida because the police became aware of her illegal activities.

For the next few years, Kathy lived in New York, Florida, Philadelphia, Detroit, and Boston. She ended up living in Jacksonville, Florida. She was still running drugs to support her drug habit and to support her lifestyle that she had grown accustomed to.

One night Kathy was on her way back to Jacksonville after running drugs through Marietta, Georgia. The police stopped her for a routine traffic stop-and-search near I-75 in Valdosta. They arrested her for drug trafficking cocaine. "I had a one quarter kilogram of cocaine (a little more than half a pound) and 400 grams of crack (about 14 ounces) in my possession," said Kathy.

Kathy served two and half years of a 20 year sentence. Kathy was then sent to Atlanta's Metro Transitional Center in July of 1999. She was glad to be there. Her friends told her that the Atlanta center was easy to live in. It didn't take Kathy long to realize she was about to have the biggest challenge of her life. She said, "All the stories I heard about MTC being a good time were lies. The truth is, it's a good-time place only if you want something for yourself.

"This place made me take a long hard look at myself. It made me decide if I wanted a good life or if I just wanted to be in and out of prison for the rest of my life. My time at MTC has been anything but easy. It's easy to take short cuts like I've done all my life. I now realize that it's just as easy to be responsible and do the right thing for myself. Yes, it's hard going out to work, then returning to the Center and still having more work to do. But this teaches me that when I am free, and I come home from work, I will still have to clean my own home. I will still have kitchen detail, but I'll have to cook and then clean up after myself. So this is just preparing me for everyday responsibilities of my life, something I didn't have time for in my past.

"I know that I am accountable for everything I do. I am tired of other people being in charge of my life. This means family, drug boys and the Department of Corrections. I don't ever want to put my life in anyone else's hands but God's. I'm willing to do whatever it takes to make this a reality."

"I sincerely believe God allowed me to survive all these trials and spared my life for a purpose. With all my past self-destructive actions, I should be dead or mentally unstable by now. I don't know the reason yet, but I believe God has allowed me to live for a reason. With His help and my determination, I'm going to make a good life for myself. My daughter and grandson deserve a healthy, safe, and happy environment, and I want to provide all of that for them."

GREW UP FAST IN PAIN
*It takes a deep commitment to change and an
Even deeper commitment to grow.*

Ralph Ellison

Emily started smoking bud when she was 10 years old. She wanted life to be like it was when she and her family lived in Chicago. She missed the closeness she had with her mother. They used to spend lots of time together and Emily had her mother's full attention. When they moved to Fort Wayne, Indiana, all of that changed.

"I was almost five years old when we moved to Fort Wayne. I didn't quite understand the move, but eventually it made sense. My father was a drug dealer and he had an opportunity to make lots of money by moving to a small city like Fort Wayne" she said. Relatives there had connections that made it easy for her father to buy and sell drugs for a lot of money.

Emily noticed changes in her mother's behavior. Her mother would stay in the bathroom often, and she would always close and lock her bedroom door. Emily said, "I found out my mother was always behind closed doors because she had developed a snorting habit. My dad, too. I never really understood why my father always used to be sleepy. I later, discovered, he was on drugs too. My parents were selling and using drugs at the same time."

Emily's parents bought her clothes and toys to keep her attention off of them. The ping pong table in her bedroom was one of Emily's favorites. She asked how her father could afford all the toys. "My dad used to tell me he always got a raise." Emily thought she had everything a child could want, but she knew, even at such a young age, that something was missing in her life. She missed her mother's love and attention.

When Emily was six, her mother had a daughter and Emily had to take care of her. By this time, drugs were affecting her mother's health. She began having nervous breakdowns. She could not take care of the two girls as she should, so Emily turned to her teachers for attention. "I used to be an attention-seeker. My teachers used to love me and I loved them." Emily found that by doing well in school, she could get attention. Nevertheless, by the time Emily was seven, her family had a bad reputation in town for dealing with drugs and students at school would tease her about her mother's breakdowns. "I don't know when the breakdowns actually started, but she would go through phases where she would leave me at home alone to watch my sister while she would go out and party. She would call me names and do things that parents don't usually do to their kids," Emily said.

By the time Emily was nine, she and her sister were staying with different family members from day to day. "Most of the time it would be Aunt Yolanda, my mother's oldest sister, but even she was doing drugs. She was just conservative about it," said Emily. When her aunt had a baby, Emily was jealous. Again, she felt neglected. "Once I got mad and sat on her baby. So I decided there was no use being jealous and found other ways of getting attention." Emily started smoking marijuana.

"My mother found some bud in my laundry and said she was going to smoke it. I was so mad with her. Out of the blue she passed the joint to me, and before I knew it my mother and I were smoking together. I finally had her attention. I thought if I kept her budded up she would be lazy and stay at home. It lasted only for a short time. I enjoyed hanging out with my mother. We had become cool except for her occasional breakdowns. We became so cool that she started smoking with a glass pipe and explained to me what it was while she cooked some free base. She even hit it in front of me and told me never to start using cocaine. I knew what cocaine was, but I didn't like it because it made my mother look scary to me." Emily said smoking marijuana with her mother made her feel close to her again. Only that didn't last too long. By the time she was 11, her parents had separated, and Emily, her mother, sister, and grandmother ended up living in Eden Green, a housing development.

Life got worse as Emily got older. By the time Emily was 13, her mother was smoking freebase crack and shooting up heroin. Her father was snorting cocaine. "I'll never forget when I was 13 and was under the care of my grandmother. When I got through riding my bike, I went home, and as I entered the basement door, I got the shock of my life. My grandmother was sitting there in the basement with a needle in her arm! Life never really was the same," she said.

Emily's Aunt Yolanda, grandmother, and father were busted in a house raid for selling drugs. Her mother was sick most of the time by then. She'd had two brain surgeries in 1990 and open- heart surgery in 1991, but she continued to use crack. Emily and her sister were on their own. To support herself and her sister, Emily started shoplifting. "I had the whole city locked down. Everybody used to place orders with me. I kept about $500 to $1000 on me every day," she said.

Emily and her sister eventually moved to California with a man who was into drugs. Within two years, their mother passed away. Emily had a daughter, and by the time her sister turned 14, she also had a baby. They all lived together for seven years.

Emily was finally beginning to believe she could accomplish something with her life. In 1993, she got a paralegal certificate. In 1994, she moved to Atlanta, not knowing the California certificate meant nothing in Georgia. "When I moved to Atlanta, I went from having a family, a car, an apartment, and jewelry to having nothing."

Again she found herself struggling to survive. Emily started making her money by selling her body, strip dancing, and selling drugs. "Boy, I made good money," she said. She still smoked marijuana but felt she had it under control. "After I started using cocaine and drinking Hennessey, smoking bud was a minor issue for me.

Emily said she eventually had regular clients to prostitute and sell drugs to. What she didn't know was one of those clients would see to it that she went to jail.

Roy befriended Emily and spent lots of money on her. She said, "he also used to smoke plenty bud. One day out of the blue, Roy paged me asking me did I know where to get some bud. I got some within a week and Roy, a friend of his, and I smoked it at my house. They liked it and asked me to get some more for them to buy. When I asked suppliers for a quarter pound of marijuana, they were skeptical at first. But I got it from them and sold it to Roy and his friend. I thought that was the end of the transaction, but that sale came back to haunt me later."

Roy and his friends were undercover police officers. "I could have kept dancing if I had known this would happen," Emily said. It was too late again. Emily was still responsible for her own two children and for her sister who had three by now.

"My greatest fear is losing time with my children while incarcerated. I also fear having ways like my family — being involved with drugs. What scares me is that I enjoy the feeling of smoking bud, and I know it leads me to self-destruction. I wonder what will happen next."

She now faces prison time because of the self-destructive decisions she made.

GOD DELIVERED ME FROM
DEAD-END RELATIONSHIPS AND DRUG

I will fear no evil for thou art with me...
Psalm 23:4

I was born in Meridian, Mississippi to Christian parents who kept me active in church. I played the piano and sang in the choir. At age 21, I left God's path and spent 12 years in what I feel was hell on earth. I was in one abusive relationship after another, each worse than the one before. I became depressed and suicidal and turned to drugs, alcohol, and sex to ease my pain. Looking back, I see that the farther away from God I got, the more worthless my life became.

I believed I was trash and that God could not possibly love someone like me. I thought I had known God my whole life but I realized that I had not known Him at all. At the deepest, darkest, lowest point in my life, I finally turned everything over to God, got off drugs and stopped drinking.

Now, when I get up each morning, I thank God for sparing me and giving me a second chance. I ask Him to show me how I can be of service to Him and to people around me. Before I go to sleep each night, I thank God for keeping me sober and filling my life with His light and love.

I WILL ALWAYS BE REMINDED OF MY DAUGHTER'S DEATH THROUGH HER CHILDREN

In this world it is not what we take up but what we give up that make us right

Henry Beecher

I lost my child, my job, and my husband all in one year. When my daughter was killed, she left behind five children — four boys and one girl. The responsibility became mine to care for them, but my husband did not want to be a part of it. He divorced me. I feel I am caught in a no win situation. I have long crying spells and I am constantly in a state of depression. I am seeking psychiatric help because sometimes I just don't want to live. I realize that I have to go on, if not for myself, then for my grandchildren.

It was a nightmare come to life. The most horrible news arrived to me on June 4, 1989 around 4 a.m. Lizzie, my oldest daughter, had been shot in the head. Hysterically, Ann, my other daughter, and I rushed to Lizzie's apartment where we saw her body lying exposed in the parking lot. By the time the ambulance arrived, Lizzie was dead. Her boyfriend had killed her while she held her 16-month-old daughter.

I have often heard that God does not give you more than you can handle. After 11 years, I know it must be true because we are still surviving. Nevertheless, what happens when people slam every door in your face when I all I wanted to do was take care of my grandchildren? I was denied social security. If I worked or had a bank account, I would not have received food stamp assistance. My home is too small for all of us. I am so concerned about one of Lizzie's sons.

He is my oldest grandson. Even though he was only six when Lizzie was killed, he has a hurt that goes deeper than I can handle. He is now 17 and under house arrest. He never could stay in the same school longer than six months. They moved him from school, but never addressed or solved his problems. They played tag with him by referring him between counselors, none ever helping him deal with his problems. His pain is so deep that only God can pull him through.

Sometimes I wonder what to do. I know God must have a plan for us.

I WAS FOUR YEARS OLD WHEN MY MOTHER WAS KILLED

Your crown has been brought and paid for. All you must do is put it on your head.

James Baldwin

I was four years old when I found my mother lying on the floor in a pool of blood. I knew what had happened. I could not stop hurting and feeling angry all the time. I went to many counseling sessions, but they did not do me any good.

My mother left five children- six, four, three, two and 16 months. My grandmother cared for us all. For a long time, my grandmother, my brothers, and sister were the only people who were real in my life. Nevertheless, I always felt angry. I wanted to stop hurting, but I did not know how. Grandmother kept us in church every Sunday, but my anger would not go away.

She allowed me to go to New Orleans with our church to a youth convention. During one session after the sermon was over, the minister said, "If you don't know God, come up to the stage." I found myself walking up on stage and when the preacher put his hand on my head, I fell to the ground. I felt heat go through my body. Something had changed inside me. I did not hurt as badly as I used to hurt.

When I returned to Atlanta and went to sleep, something awakened me. I saw my mother standing at the door of my room. It frightened me at first, but when she smiled at me, I knew everything would be alright. She then disappeared.

I sometimes get angry and I don't know why I cannot control my feelings. I deal with this behavior through a youth program that teaches singing and acting. My instructor told me that acting is one way to work anger out. I know I have a long way to go, but I also know that with God, I can do all things through Christ who strengthens me.

HURTING INSIDE

You cannot belong to anyone else, until you belong to yourself.

PEARL BAILEY

My daddy used drunkenness as an excuse for raping me and my girlfriend when she spent the night with me one night. My girlfriend and I both pretended it didn't happen, but later, with her eyes filled with tears, she told me what my daddy did to her.

Years before this when I was five years old, my grandmother and I used to drink beer together. She allowed me to curse and we never went to church. As I grew older, I was in and out of detention homes.

By 11, I had lost my virginity to a 12 year-old boy. I thought sex was what made him happy. When I was 13, I thought I was in love with the man of my dreams. I allowed him to abuse me mentally and physically. I thought that was how boys showed their love.

Then walk in was my daddy. My girlfriend slept over one night and the unthinkable happened. While she slept on the couch and I slept on the love seat, she told me that my daddy came into the room and raped her and threaten her not to yell. What I didn't know was that she pretended to be asleep when she heard my daddy come back into the room and rape me, his own daughter. I didn't know she had seen it all. I was too ashamed to mention it to her until she confessed to me what he had done to her.

The next day my daddy took us shopping. He apologized for what he had done, saying he wasn't himself. My girlfriend and I realized at that moment that he had raped both of us in the same night.

At 16 I moved to North Carolina with my aunt. This proved to be a safe environment. I pray that if you or anyone you know has experienced abuse of any kind please tell somebody and get help for yourself or them.

WHO CARES ABOUT MY PAIN?

Your attitude about who you are and what you have is a very little thing that makes a very big difference.

THEODORE ROOSEVELT

Watching my mother in one bad relationship after another has left me clear of what are good and bad relationships. I have never known what motherly love is or what it feels like to have a mother's love. My mother never grew up.

Some things have happened to me that I have not shared with anyone. I know I need to let these bottled-up feelings outside my body in order to start healing. I have often wanted to tell someone, but I could never bring myself to do so. As I sit in my apartment bedroom with only a bed and two lamps, and my clothes still packed in plastic bags sitting against the walls, tears run down my face with shame just thinking about my life. My family depends on me to be the strong one, to keep their lives on track. They never stop to think of my struggles, my heartaches and my pains.

I am 17 years old and was born on December 5th. But I feel like I am 71 by the experiences I have gone through all my life. As I sit here, I pray that with God's help, I am able to tell about my experiences of abuse.

I have no remembrances of having the love of my mother-not the unconditional love every child deserves to have from birth. My mother had three children by the time she was 16. Being a child herself when I was born, my mother never had time to develop motherly love.

She was trying to find love in all the wrong places. All our children's fathers were in their 50s. She had no interest in school. She dropped out in 10th grade. My mother expected these older men to support her, but in the end, they all dropped her. She always fell back on her welfare checks.

I saw my mother go through many relationships. None lasted. She would sometimes leave us home alone, and when she was out of town, she would leave us in the care of our grandmother, her mother.

I still have a scar on my hand from the time I was six months old and became dehydrated because we had no air or fans in the house. The I.V. was inserted in my hand improperly, which caused it to swell. My mother thought I was dead because my body became cold. Luckily, I turned out all right with a scar on my left hand and I only had to wear a brace until it healed. That medical center in Athens, Georgia was sued, and from what my grandmother told me, I was supposed to receive a lump sum of money when I turned 18. That never happened. My mother spent it all.

By the time I was two years old, my mother had five children. Tee was the father of two of them. He would beat my mother in front of us. I thought it would be better for my mother when we moved in with Tee, but things got worse. He would have other women over while my mother was not home. And by the time I was four years old, night after night, Tee would come into our bedroom and fondle us, even my brother. He would play in our vaginas and rub my little brother's penis.

I felt sad, helpless, and scared. I finally told my grandmother what Tee was doing. "That bastard is going to pay for this!" my grandmother shouted. When she told my mother about this, my mother said, "Why don't you mind your own business and stay the hell out of mine? That damned girl is telling lies. Now don't call my house no more." My mother cursed at her mother a lot, but she would always end up needing her again. This time was no exception. They would stop talking for a while, and then my mother would eventually need my grandmother who was always willing to help us.

My mother never believed me when I told her how her boyfriends would fondle me or has intercourse with me until one day she caught Tee standing over my bed. She had no choice but to believe what I had been telling her. And although she depended on Tee to take care of us financially, my mother chased him out of the house with a butcher knife. She apologized to me for not believing me, and she apologized to her mother also. My grandmother allowed us to live with her until my mother could afford her own place. My grandmother never turned her back on us.

I was sure we would have a safer life when my mother got her own apartment. But my mother was still living the life of the teenager she never got a chance to be since starting her family so young. She had three friends- Jewel, Barbara, and Gidget – with whom children who did horrible things to us.

They beat us, made us parade in front of them naked, and poured hot water on us. They would lock us in their dirty clothes hampers. They threatened to hurt us if we ever told, so we did not tell. We just pleaded with our mother not to leave us with Jewel's children. But she would not listen to us. All she wanted was to go out and have fun.

One night when she left us there, Jewel's 19-year-old son raped me. I was six years old. He took me in the bathroom, unbuckled his belt and zipped down his pants with smiling at me. In the back of my mind was, "Why is he undressing in front of me? "Put your whole mouth on my penis, he said. So I did. I was so afraid. He told me to suck his penis and swallow it. I tried so hard until I vomited. He said, "Let's put some toothpaste on my penis to make it better for you." I was crying and anxious to leave the bathroom. He took me into his bedroom, undressed me, and laid me on his bed, kissing and touching me and rubbing his penis against my vagina.

My trouble didn't stop there. When I was seven, my mother met and married Eli, another abusive man. She started going to church, but never dressed us as nicely as she dressed. She made Eli her priority. My mother would fix Eli's food first and then fix food for her children.

Eli never wanted us to go into the refrigerator after dark. If he caught us in the refrigerator, he would beat us back to our beds. He became more abusive. He would argue about the simplest things. Whenever he felt like it, he would make me pull down my clothes and placed his foot across my back and beat me until he was tired.

Eli did not have a license to drive. We were on our way to Florida when he was arrested for driving without a license. As usual, my mother was dependent on this man to support us. When he got arrested he could not pay the bond.

My mother started spending less time with us, and was in and out of different relationships again. My baby sister and brother would stay at the carwash all day begging for quarters while I sometimes sat on the sidewalk at night begging for money.

While Eli was in jail, my mom dated Will and let him move in with us. Eli found out about that and she lost both of them.

Then came Jo, a lesbian with a son name John. Jo was on drugs. My mother let them move in with us. I was nine years old. John would play games with my sister and me by having us take turns sitting on his lap. My sister had enough sense to run away when she realized what John was doing. I stayed. One time he laid me on the bed and tried to force his penis inside my vagina. I told him, "Stop! Stop! That hurts. Please stop." "Open your legs and relax," he told me, and so when I did, his penis slid right into my vagina. This abuse lasted for months and I told no one. Some nights I would wake and find him in my bed. I never told my mother because she never talked to me. She was always in her room behind closed doors with Jo.

To support her drug habit, Jo had all of us, including my mother, stealing for her. She became abusive and would beat us and my mother. One day, when I was being teased by some children in the neighborhood about my mother being a lesbian, I ran into the house crying to tell my about it. But when I opened the bedroom door, I found her and Jo making love. Jo realized I was standing there and later she came to my room and beat me for having opened the door. My mother never came to defend me.

Then came Thomas, "Mr. Fix-it," who claimed he could fix anything. He was supposed to fix our washing machine, but he ended up fixing me. One night as I was asleep, Thomas awakened me asking if I would go to the store with him. It was 2 a.m. Instead he took me to the kitchen and started kissing my face and neck. He sat me on top of the washing machine, and pulled down my nightgown and panties. As he rubbed his penis inside my vagina, I told him to stop. When he did stop, afraid, I ran into my bedroom and lay down. I never told anyone.

I have been sexually and mentally abused as long as I can remember. My mother's friends abused me and my friends abused me. I learned from the streets than from anywhere else. I remember all these things happening to me as if it were yesterday.

With tears still running down my face, I beg God to help me begin the healing process. I realized healing is a long process, but I know with God's help, all things are possible.

My heart is pounding like a drummer boy beating his drum. My tears soaked my bed like rain wetting the grass, killing a hot summer's day. I have learned that a wise man learns from others' mistakes. I ask for your prayers.

CHAPTER 3

WOUNDED HEARTS

There must be inner healing for the broken vessel.
Rev. Linda Hollies

No matter what
hurt or pain you
are facing today
there is a way
out of it.
Look inside
that pain or hurt,
face it head on.

She spent her two days making her outfit, spent her last $50 on a new pair of shoes. She had her hair and nails done, spent 45 minutes putting on her makeup. When she got there, she spent the entire evening sitting in the comer, half smiling, half crying. On the outside she looked beautiful. On the inside she felt worthless. So many of us invest a fortune making ourselves look good to the world, yet on the inside we are falling apart. We manage to muddle through life saying and doing the right things, but when we're alone we cry silent and desperate tears. It time to pause and heal the inside. It is time to heal the hurts, mend the fences, dig up the hatchets and throw them away. It is time to heal the doubts, answer the questions and release the fears. It is time to invest some time to what is going on inside. When we can do that, the outside will shine.

Acts of Faith,

Iyanla Vanzant

THIRTY-SEVEN AND WISER

My experiences have made me wiser and more productive woman. I have allowed my past experiences to help me mature into good decision-maker. I have been through many problems, but at 37 years old, I feel I have learned how to survive the wounds that are in my heart.

I learned that hurt extends beyond sexual and physical abuses. Looking back on my childhood, I realize there were many self-inflicted wounds, and were inflicted on me by others. I did not recognize the hurt as a child because I did not know it was pain. As a teenager, I caused much of my own hurt and pain. If I had it in my mind to do something, no one could tell me differently. I would do it no matter who got hurt. Of course, I always suffered the consequences, but the consequences did not get my attention. As a 37-year-old adult, some of my childhood decisions haunt me now and I am paying attention.

Childhood

As a child I was taught to obey adults. Not to do so was cause for punishment. When I was eight years old, I remember playing with my uncle's son who was in his 20s. His playing was different from mine, but because he was an adult, I did whatever he asked me to do. I thought if I told, no one would believe me. I asked myself who I could turn to. In my young mind, the answer was no one. So the next time he raped me, my mind told me to shut up and do what I was told. I was just supposed to do what adults told me to do or I would get in trouble. Little did I know of the wounds that were being embedded.

Middle School

The older I got, the more I thought I knew about life. No one could tell me anything that I did not want to hear. I had been through so much as a child; I thought I knew everything there was to know about life, especially about relationships with me.

I was a troublemaker at school. And when I had to get counseling, what do you think happened? Instead of sending me to a school counselor, one of my teachers decided to do the counseling himself. He convinced me that all I needed was some attention. We began an affair, and I allowed it to continue for years. I thought I was being fulfilled with whatever was missing in my life, but I was wrong. I was only covering up hurts and making the pain worse.

As I think back, I know what I put myself through was disgusting and sickening. I told no one, but the wounds inside me were wide open. Who could I tell? No one.

During my teen years, I felt a lot of self-pity. I felt that everyone picked on me. If someone needed blaming for something, it was I they blamed. The seed was planted. I grew up with that mentality. Because I allowed this self-pity to grow in me, I grew more selfish and defiant. I kept everything to myself-everything I did to myself and everything others did to me. No one would care anyway.

High School

My pace of knowing everything was at all-time high. I knew what love was and I knew I would find the love of my life. Lots of boys were interested in me, and I liked them, too. I fell in love, but our relationship was purely sexual for him. This should have been a hint for me to leave the relationship, but my heart told me differently.

Others tried telling me, but I would not listen. No one else could tell me anything. He did not have to trick me into having sex with him because I knew what I was doing. I got pregnant and he got lost. Although I lost the baby due to complications with the pregnancy, I think for the first time I felt hurt, heartbroken, disappointed, and angry. I was in love with him, but he did not love me. I still did not see the picture. All I knew was that I was feeling something I had never felt before.

Young Adult

After I lost the baby, I felt my life was a disaster. I committed myself to the church. I knew I could find whatever it was I was looking for in the church. Surely I could depend on the church. I thought I could find peace in the church. But instead some church people accused me of interfering in marriages.

My stubbornness reared its ugly head. To strike back, I began to have relationships with men in the church, whether they were married or not. It did not matter because they were accusing me of it anyway. And that time, it was true. This continued until I had enough of the bad talk about me.

One day I went to two men in leadership positions in the church. They counseled me, showed me how to start believing in myself. Whenever I needed a boost or was feeling down, I could contact them. No matter how hard I tried to straighten out my life, rumors continued about me in the church. I was grateful for their help. But I was blindsided when one of them approached me to show my gratitude through sex. Who could I turn to? Nobody but Jesus.

At 37, that is behind me. Looking over my life, I know what I did was wrong and was not in good favored with God. I know I still need healing and I ask for your prayers for my complete healing or these old wounds and for my continued success as I struggle to live a life that is good in God's eyes.

A STORY OF HIDDEN PAIN

If you met me, you wouldn't know my pain. I hide it real well. I believe pain is a weakness.

I have a beautiful daughter who is studying to receive her master's degree in social science. She's always asking me questions. A week ago she asked me what my earliest memory as a child was. I told her about what I thought of my father's leaving, my last memory.

To this day, I'm still not sure if that memory was of my father. I remember my mother giving me a bath in a yellow tub and my father giving me a banana-flavored Popsicle before he left. I didn't see my father again until I was 18 years old. We were at his mother funeral. He did not even know me. His sister took me to him and introduced me. He said, "Oh yeah. How you doing?" Then he commented on how I had messed up my life, according to his sister.

To my knowledge, my stepfather came into my life at an early age. I particularly remember the early days. He was a quiet, strong man, a hunter and a fisherman. I always felt his muscles as he was shaving for work.

My mother and stepfather would take us to my stepbrothers and step sisters' house on the weekend sometimes. Mother would cook grits in the morning, press the girls' hair, and my stepfather would whip the children.

When we were left alone with him, the sexual molestation took place. My mother worked at the main post office on the first shift and my stepfather worked the second shift. If the house was not cleaned by the time mother came in, I was awakened because I was the middle child and the oldest daughter.

We all had alternate days of being responsible for making sure the house was kept in order. My brother thought it was women's work and my sister was just lazy and did not care if the house was clean, so it fell back on me. If they did not take their turn to clean I would usually be up late at night and my stepfather would find me and ask me to come downstairs with him.

He would tell me, "I'll make your breasts grow big if I feel on them." In my mind I'm thinking, "What do I care?" But it never felt right. I made an excuse to get away from him the first time. After that night, I slept with my bedroom door locked. Sometimes I would not be finished cleaning, but when I heard him coming up those stairs, I would lock my door.

He would knock on the door sometimes and ask if I needed some help. I knew what he meant. I would say no. I hid from him a lot. He would come up behind me and grab my breasts while I was washing dishes, even while my brother was in the house. This went on for all my teenage years.

All of my family got together for the holidays and family reunions. We would take long trips to upper Wisconsin on the weekends. We were a close and loving family. We would go to church with my grandmother, but my mother and stepfather were not regular churchgoers.

I gave birth to a daughter at the age of 20. I moved out of my mother's house about 18 months later. But I always worried when my daughter went to my parents' house for the weekend. I wondered if my child was safe around this man. I always watched my stepfather when he would pick her up to make sure that he was not touching her inappropriately.

When I was in my 20s, my stepfather started selling drugs. He coerced my daughter's father into that lifestyle. But you have to understand that my stepfather was a very lovable, quiet man and one of those older gentlemen who always had a story, and you never knew if it was true or false.

One time I got high with him, my sister, and my cousin. The only reason I did it was because I was considered to be sort of nerdy. They would say if I did it one time, I wouldn't be able to stop. Not true. I never touched it again.

I took a moment to try to talk to my stepfather about how I did not like him touching and grabbing at me. I thought he understood, but his behavior continued when I would visit my mother. I knew in my heart I truly loved him, but he did not understand me.

I lost my apartment and had to move back home. My mother helped me fix the basement to make it livable. That man would grab my body parts every chance he got, mostly when I was washing dishes.

Finally, I tried to tell my mother. She seemed not to believe me. So I told my grandmother. She said, "We don't talk about things like that." I went to my uncle and he told me I needed to be ashamed of myself for talking about this with him.

I talked to my child's father about my abuse, but my stepfather was his buddy. I felt feelings were not addressed. There was a lot of miscommunication in our relationship after that. Through no fault of my boyfriends' I had issues. Depending on how he would approach me, I would go off on him. I could not stand for anyone to come up behind me.

My boyfriend was my one and only love, and l lost him. He's married to someone else and now I am sad. I want what I can't have. I don't trust men. What do they want from me? They say I am pretty but I don't see that. I look in the mirror every day, and I miss the beauty that other people see.

Today, I am getting my life back together. I have a good job and my own apartment. I am learning to love myself. I go to counseling sessions. I am in church and learning more about myself. Today I am pleased with what I see in me.

WOUNDED HEARTS

*PEOPLE
BECOME
HOMELESS,
HURT AND
WOUNDED IN
THE MIND
LONG BEFORE
THEY ACT IT
OUT ON THE
STREET.*

There are times when we feel bad about ourselves, what we've done and what we are facing. In these moments we may even believe we deserve to be punished, because we are "bad" or have done bad things. There are times when we feel so low, we convince ourselves that we don't matter and neither does anything or anyone else. That is when we usually start to think about God. Is there such a thing? Does God really care? Maybe if we had gone to God before, we wouldn't be where we are now. No matter. We're here, so let's go. This is a prime opportunity to make a new start, begin again, and move on. The key is to remember that no matter where we've been, what we've done or how awful we feel right now, the One we may be running from knows exactly where we are. He has placed a light of peace in our hearts. A prayer will flip the switch.

Acts of Faith,

Iyanla Vanzant

I AM AN HURTING BLACK MALE

I am a hurting black male who has been wounded by the incest in my family while I was growing up. It started with my grandfather. For years, he sexually molested two of his own biological daughters. They had sons by their father. This incestuous relationship was only the beginning of a family tradition.

DAUGHTER NO. 1

Years after leaving my hometown, I learned that one of my grandfather's sons, my cousin, molested his daughters. Once while my cousin was having sex with his daughter, his son entered the room and saw what his father was doing. My cousin beat his son and threatened to hurt him if he ever told anyone. This incestuous relationship continued for years until the daughter left home for college. The son never was the same.

My cousin's son began stealing and using drugs because he could not cope with his father molesting his sisters and not being able to tell anyone. He didn't know how to deal with his hurt. He wanted to kill his father, but in his heart he knew that was wrong.

He was unable to punish his father, so he acted out his hurt by stealing. He was arrested and spent time in prison. He finally had the opportunity to tell someone what his father was doing. He wrote to his aunts about what he had seen, and that he could not bear not telling anyone since his father had threatened him. He apologized for the trouble he had caused them, but knew of no other way to release his pain other than to kill his father.

DAUGHTER NO. 2

As my cousin's second daughter approached her teen years, he began molesting her. She was stronger than the older daughter and decided to resist him. She told her sister what their father was doing to her. Her sister confided in the younger sister that he had also molested her for many years. The younger reported the molestation to the authorities, but they took no action because my cousin was an upstanding deacon in the church. Back then, a girl's word was never taken over her parent's word.

DAUGHTER NO. 3

Unfortunately, my cousin was not afraid of being punished. He began molesting his youngest daughter. She was younger than her sisters when they were molested. All the other children were on their own now and she did not stand a chance. The molestation went on for years and she had a child by him. She began acting out her hurt by being promiscuous. This lifestyle hurt her father, only because he was a deacon in the church and he worried what people would say. The people of the church saw what she was doing and wondered why this was happening, but no one questioned him.

WOUNDED HEARTS

I am a hurting black male and I found that there are many like me that are hurting. In my family there is a spirit of lust that causes the men to act out through sex, cocaine, and crack. This lustful spirit does not end because a person receives Jesus Christ in his life. Some of us need an engrafted word to save our minds. It is only through the word of God that this can happen. We must fill that space with the power of God's love and his word.

Wounds come in many forms:

When I was a pastor of a congregation in Alabama in 1986, I remember thinking that people who live on the streets, in shelters, or people who live from house to house wanted to be homeless. Little did I know that I would experience homelessness first hand. God showed me that homelessness is not something one chooses, but is a transition in life.

My heart ached when my mother died in 1991. I was the strong one in the family, the pastor. I eulogized my mother and never shed a tear because I wasn't expected to cry. My family expressed their pain through crying, but I didn't cry until months later. At the time of my mother's death, my marriage was in trouble so I didn't have time to let my guard down. I didn't realize how serious my marriage problems were.

Three months after my mother's death, my wife left me for another man. The pain opened a wound I thought would never close. My heart became cold and I stopped doing what I knew was right. I felt sorry for myself and decided to never trust anyone again.

If that wasn't enough, my right hip was deteriorating and it was hard for me to walk. It became impossible for me to work. At this point, I found out what homeless actually meant.

The next thing I knew I was living in a place that was temporary because I had nowhere to go. I was homeless. The pain overtook me and I could not focus on reality. I couldn't work because I began to have mental problems. I knew God was still leading me because I found the energy to volunteer in community centers for the homeless. I could help others, but I could not help myself.

My right hip got worse, and I had major surgery to replace it. Two months after surgery, I found myself struggling to maintain permanent housing because of having no income.

Through all of this, God was still guiding me. There were others in worse shape than me. My issues were mild compared to other homeless people. Most of all, it broke my heart to see homeless mothers with children living in shelters and under bridges. I saw lot of despair in men who turned to alcohol and drugs to ease their pain.

Survival comes from within a person. I recognized that people become homeless, hurt, and wounded in their minds long before they act it out on the street or destroy someone else.

We go through hurts and pains, but God shows us a brighter future. No matter what pain or hurt you are facing today, there is a way out of it.

CHAPTER 4

"THE SOLUTION"

In the next section, the messages serve to help us heal. Look inside your pain or hurt and face it head on.

Far too many children as well as adults have suffered through the kinds of abuses you have just read about. It is a sad and tragic thing. What is more sad is that even if or when the abuse stops, even when the body heals, the abused person often lives out their entire life in the same hell mentally they were in when they were being physically abused. People often spend so much time and energy trying to figure out why these things happened to them in the first place and are not taught how to get beyond their past. They do not know how to let it go. Most of us have unpleasant things to some degree or another, some worse than others, from our childhood or our teen years or as young adults that we still carry around with us and we would like to forget it and make it go away but we do not know how or we do not think it even possible to rid ourselves from the memory of the person or the events that caused us so much pain.

Many, who have suffered from abuse, whether mental, emotional or physical, will turn to some type of substance such as drugs or alcohol or even food to cover up the pain. When we suffer pain or unhappiness, we tend to reach for something on the outside of us to solve the problem. Not only does this not solve the problem but it creates another problem. We become mentally and sometimes physically addicted to something else that will bring us pain and suffering. We spend a lot of time and money and energy on things to make us feel better. And maybe some of those things do make us feel better for a short period of time in the beginning. Anyone who has been involved in substance abuse knows that the drug or the alcohol or the overeating or whatever they choose to use to cover their pain wears off and they begin to use more and after a while it just does not work for them. To pretend that something is working is a lie. We lie to ourselves when we say that we use anything to make us feel better when, in fact, it is destroying our lives. We just trade one kind of misery for another. Many live their lives in constant guilt and a feeling of unworthiness because of their past and they punish themselves by their lifestyle and they allow others to take advantage of them in many ways.

There are many stories in the beginning of this book that tell of appalling acts of people on others. The most obvious questions people usually ask themselves is, "How could anyone do this type of abuse to another person, especially a child?" and "Why would they do it?" The single most important thing to remember about anyone and everyone is this: People always behave according to the way they think. It is not the actions of a person that is the cause of the problem. A person's way of thinking is always the cause of the way they behave or respond. The Bible teaches us in Proverbs 23:7 "As a man thinketh in his heart, so is he." This is a law or principle of life and we are all subject to this law. It is like the law of gravity, it affects us all the same way no matter what kind of person we are. This has been the truth since the beginning of time but mankind has only just begun to understand it. We are finally realizing that our thoughts control our actions.

A person who is an abuser of any kind has a certain way of thinking that causes them to behave or respond to someone else the way they do. It is wrong and it is inexcusable but chances are their way of thinking is a result of how they were raised and the kind of things they were taught. We are all taught by our parents and those adults we grow up with how to think. They do not necessarily teach us with words, they teach us with their attitudes and their actions. Children learn much more from their parent's attitudes than from what they are told. What children are told often 'goes in one ear and out the other' if it is not supported by the way their parents really are. If you tell a child it is wrong to be angry but yet you are always angry, the child will learn to be angry no matter what you have said. This is true in all areas of life. A parent will shape the way a child grows up to be. If a child learns to be like the parent, and they continue in the same direction of attitude that their parents have, they typically take that attitude a step farther. A child, as he or she grows up, will be more severe in his way of thinking than the parents were. This results in more severe actions and responses. Often times, generation after generation only gets worse and worse in some families.

It is not uncommon for a person who is abused as a child to become an abuser when they have children of their own. However, this is not always the case because we all reserve the right and have the responsibility to use our own free will. We have an opportunity at all times to make changes in ourselves by making changes in our way of thinking. We can choose to have a positive attitude or a negative attitude no matter what we have been through. Someone who is an abuser to self or to others and continues to be that way is refusing to accept the gift that God gave us all – a choice. None of us are forced to behave in a bad or harmful way. We choose our behavior by our own thinking. There is no justification for negative and harmful behavior. This is true for the abused as well as the abuser. People who have been abused, whether mentally, emotionally or physically are also subject to the law of thought. Many who grow up in an abusive atmosphere feel helpless and hopeless as a child and grow into angry and violent adults. They have learned to be angry and violent because they grew up with angry and violent people. They continue in the helpless and hopeless way of thinking. Many believe they cannot change because the fear and anger in them has become such a part of their being that is all they can see and feel. Many of those who have been abused and are filled with bitterness and anger have never even considered trying to make a change in them. They just are the way they are and that is the way it is. Those who feel this way are continuing the abuse cycle; they are abusing themselves for sure and possibly others. To live in an attitude of bitterness and anger and fear always results in negative and harmful behavior.

There comes a time when you have to say, "Enough!" Stop the vicious cycle of pain and guilt and stop lying to yourself. There is a way out of this kind of thinking. Do not allow others to keep you convinced you have to remain the same because you don't! You are a powerful being because you were created in the image of God. God created you to create for yourself a life of abundance; abundant joy, abundant peace, abundant happiness, abundance of anything you want. The only thing that will stop the flow of abundance in your life is your own thinking.

Many people who are abusers are that way because they were abused themselves, they were trained a certain way to think by their parents or some other adult. We always grow up thinking the way our parents thought because that is what we know. We have tendencies like those who raised us. It may not always be so obvious to us because we say all our lives things like, "I'll never be like my mother or my father!" That statement right there is a sure sign that you will be very much like your mother or your father. You may not understand how this can be true but you are going to learn a lot about your thinking in this book. The information you will learn here about yourself is life transforming and can and will set you free if you will accept it and put it into practice. Remember, to practice something does not mean to do it one time; it means to continue to do it.

If you want to change your life, you must change your thinking. The apostle Paul told us in Romans 12:2, "...be transformed by the renewing of your mind..." To transform outside circumstances and events we must first transform the inside, our mind. How do we do it?

FIRST STEP

Become willing to change. Sometimes we are so bound to our own way of thinking and living and even though we do not like it, we are familiar with it, we
know what to expect, even though we are not happy. We are afraid of any kind of change. We often are afraid because we feel like we are not going to be in control anymore. We do not want to rock the boat because it might get worse and out of control, we continue to believe things are just fine the way they are. To be willing to change is simply a matter of choice. The word "will" means a determination or a desire. Your will is your power. Your will is what you determine you are going to do. When you determine to do something, it is an absolute solid decision and there is nothing that will stop you from completing the act. When we are not willing to change our minds or the way we believe, we are using our willpower to remain where we are in our life. We are determined to stay in a suffering state. Where we are in our lives is always our choice. We can choose to be 'willing' or to be 'willful'. There is a huge difference! To be willing is to give up our own way of being and be ready to accept something better. It is a positive determination to learn a new way to better ourselves and our lives. To be willful is to continue to live according to our own will. It involves our own reasoning. Being willful is being stubborn and rebellious. If we refuse to budge from where we are we will continue to experience the same kind of life we want to change.

To know and understand that we are mental beings and not just physical beings is what liberates us. We remain in bondage as long as we believe we are just physical beings. Our bondage is our mental atmosphere, our habits of thought. We can never change our environment without changing our habits of thought. "As within, so without". The way we think on the inside will always manifest on the outside.

When we were children we did not understand this and we did not really make a choice how to think, we just followed the way of our parents or other adults we grew up with. This does not always mean we always do exactly the same things they did, but it does mean we were so strongly influenced by them that we tend to be like them in many ways. If our parents were bitter and angry, if they hated certain people and were blamers and condemners and always complaining about things, we probably have a tendency to be the same way to a certain extent, sometimes we are even more extreme in some areas than our parents. If we are honest with ourselves we know this is true. We often hear this: "I can't help it that is the way I was raised." Why do we let the way we were raised control our lives? There is no rule or law that says you cannot change. In fact there is a law that says you can change and even commands you to change. Jesus Christ said in Mark 12:30-31, "And thou shalt love the Lord thy God with all thy heart, and with all thy soul, and with all thy mind and with all thy strength. This is the first commandment. And the second is like, namely this, thou shalt love thy neighbor as thyself. There is none other commandment greater than these."

Jesus would not give us a command that we could not follow. In order to be obedient in these commands there is a second step we must take.

SECOND STEP

We must forgive. Wow! That is a huge step for some because of the things they have experienced. How could you possibly forgive someone who has done such horrible things to you or who has treated you so awful and they never even apologized or even acknowledged their actions? This may be a really big step for you but know this: It is an absolutely necessary step. Without forgiveness your life will never change for the better, it will only get worse. This is a fact that not one of us can change. It is the law of life. Like produces like. Unforgiveness produces unforgiveness. Matthew 6:14-15 tells us,"For if ye forgive men their trespasses, your heavenly Father will also forgive you, but if ye forgive not men their trespasses, neither will your Father forgive your trespasses." This is the law or principle Jesus taught. Luke 6-37 says,"Judge not, and ye shall not be judged, condemn not and ye shall not be condemned. Forgive and ye shall be forgiven." When this law is understood as the law of your mind, you can let go of your past and continue on to a brighter future without the weight of the pain and misery you have been carrying around with you. You can live free and will not feel the need to depend on substances or circumstances to control your emotional state. You can allow the power inside you to create happiness. You can will to be free from your past.

The forgiveness step also applies to forgiving yourself. Often people who are abused live in guilt because they believe it is their own fault. Living in guilt is destructive. Many people are encouraged by others to feel guilt, they are blamed and they blame themselves. It is common for abusers to try to make their victims feel guilty and worthless, as though they deserve to be punished.

Many people claim they love God but they live in a state of hatred and unforgiveness of someone or themselves. It is not possible to love God if you do not love and forgive another no matter what they have done to you. I John 4:20 states, "If a man say, I love God, and hateth his brother, he is a liar: for he that loveth not his brother whom he hath seen, how can he love God whom he hath not seen?" Now, who is your brother? Anyone and everyone. You cannot love God with all your heart, soul, mind and strength without loving others and yourself as well. We do not have to agree with the actions and lifestyles of others but we must love them. We do not have to invite them into our homes or even allow them there but we must love them. We do not have to be involved in the lives of those who have hurt us, but we must love them. We do not do it because they deserve love; we do it so that we can receive love. We give love so that we receive love. Love is our birthright; God gives us love because that is what God is. God is love. It is up to us to receive it and there is only one way to make that happen. We always get in return what we give. We must give love to receive love. We must give forgiveness in order to receive forgiveness. God always loves us and forgives us. It is up to us to receive it.

The third step is so closely related to the second that it is almost the same step.

THIRD STEP

We must let go. When we forgive someone, at that point we are letting go of the hatred and anger and bitterness and resentment we have been holding onto. We are learning to love others without condition. We must also let go of the memories of past events and practice replacing those thoughts with good thoughts. The negative thoughts we have concerning people from our past who have hurt us bring pain and we want to achieve a state of peace. Philippians 4:7-8 says,"And the peace of God, which passes all understanding, shall keep your hearts and minds through Christ Jesus. Finally, brethren, whatsoever things are *true*, whatsoever things are *honest*, whatsoever things are *just*, whatsoever things are *pure*, whatsoever things are *lovely*, whatsoever things are of *good report*, if there be any *virtue*, and if there be any *praise*, *think on these things*." The Bible teaches us that our power to change is in our mind. We are to choose the thoughts that will bring peace and joy and happiness. If we want to be happy, we must think happy. If we want peace in our lives, then we must think peace. Only then will we create happy and peaceful circumstances. This is how it works. This is what Jesus taught. What we think is what we get. How we think is how we are. We have the choice to remain the same or to make great changes. It is all up to us.

You are the person you think you are. What you think is what you believe and the longer you think it the more you attract the kind of things into your life you are thinking. If you think you are unworthy, then you will speak and act that way. If you think you are stupid then you will speak and act that way. If you think all your troubles, whether they be financial or relationship issues or health or anything else, are someone else's fault then you will speak and act that way. If you continue to think you are a victim then you will continue to speak and act that way. If you think you are confident, then you will speak and act that way. If you think you are valuable then you will speak and act that way.

You are exactly what you believe you are and evidence of that is your life. Take a close look at the way you handle your money. Are you paying all your bills? Do you pay them when they are due? Do you spend money when you should be saving? Do you spend money on things you do not need or things you never use? Does it seem like you never have enough money? Consider your relationships with other people. Is there something about almost everyone you know that really bugs you? Do you wonder why so many people are this way? Do you get irritated or angry with others easily? Does it appear to you that almost all your problems are someone else's fault? Do you have peaceful and trusting relationships with others or do all your relationships seem dysfunctional? How many times have you broken up with someone or has someone broken up with you? Does it always seem to be pretty much for the same reasons? Do you have a happy and peaceful marriage? How is your relationship with your family members? Do you have an illness that will not go away? Do you get sick every year with colds or flu? Does it seem like you get a lot of injuries? Are you always in a depressed state? Are you happy or unhappy? Not handling your money well, bad relationships, blaming others for your problems, poor health and depression are all symptoms, they are not the problem.

Even though you may have experienced unspeakable acts for which there is no excuse from the hands of someone else, someone who was supposed to be your protector and instead they were your worst nightmare. Even though your body and spirit have been damaged, you can be healed from these painful scars. But you must make the choice to make your life different, to make your life better. No one else can do it for you. You are always making a choice whether you realize it or not. If you do not choose to improve your life then you are choosing not to make a change and your life will remain the same as it is now and may even get worse. Making a change is an active event. The activity takes place in your thoughts. To change your life you must take action in your own mind. You must change your thoughts concerning the events from your past. You have not become the person you are today because of something that has happened to you in the past. You are who you are because of what you think about the things that occurred in your life or the person or persons who have hurt you and what you think about yourself. Even though you have experienced pain and suffering in your life, you do not have to stay there in your mind. You can change your life by changing your thoughts. You *must* change your thoughts; it is the only way out.

How do I change my thoughts? If you have asked yourself that question, then you have already made a giant leap in your thinking. At least you are considering the fact that you can change the way you think. It may seem like an impossible task, but it is not. No doubt, it requires practice and patience. We must become determined to make a change.

By nature we are habitual thinkers. The kinds of thoughts we dwell in today are the kind of thoughts we have been trained to think. We grow up thinking like those around us and it just feels so natural and right we usually defend our way of thinking and believe if others don't think like we do then there is something wrong with them. Many times we know people who are happy and well-adjusted and successful and we don't like them because they do not get angry with people who wrong them the way we would or they will not try to get revenge and we just don't understand why. Some people simply cannot stand to be around others who are happy and peaceful and full of joy. This state of mind is so unfamiliar to them it makes them uncomfortable. We even hear sarcastic remarks about happy people such as, 'They aren't living in the real world!' or 'They wouldn't be so happy if they knew what was really going on!' or 'They do not know what real pain and suffering is.'

The truth is that many people who are happy and joyful have experienced much pain and suffering in their lives, often more than you or I can imagine. Evidence declares that throughout time many people have overcome all kinds of adversity and changed their lives by not allowing their circumstances to control them but they learned to control their circumstances. They did this by creating for themselves a new way of thinking. Someone once said, "Holding onto grievances is a decision to suffer." We so often chain ourselves to the most horrible memories of our past as though it is something we treasure, something we cherish. These memories become our identity. There is a man whose name is Tony, who, from the time he was born, mostly lived in an atmosphere of alcohol and drugs. He never knew his father and his young mother was more interested in herself than she was in him. She allowed things and events and certain people into her life that were extremely detrimental. Tony experienced mental abuse and a certain degree of physical abuse. He is 37 years old today. He left home at 16 and has been involved in drugs and alcohol and much criminal activity, been in jail many times. He has been homeless many times; he has been in several drug and alcohol rehab centers. Tony lost a wife and a child to divorce, has lost cars and trucks and jobs and all other kinds of things. He is bitter and angry and always has been. From the time he was in kindergarten throughout his life, he has been violent and angry. He is still that way today. Tony lives his life identifying with his past. He blames all his problems on his mother and others. He lives his life with the belief that he is not successful because of his past. He surrounds himself with the same kind of people, those who think like him. He has the ability to change his life; he is very intelligent and handsome. He has tried on many occasions to become a better person, to hold a job, to be married, to look better, to dress better, etc. He has been and may still be addicted to crack cocaine. The problem is that he has not let go of the past. His attempts at change have only been on the outside. Real change begins on the inside. Tony refuses forgiveness. He will not give it nor will he receive it. He has not forgiven himself or others. He believes he has a right to be angry about the things he experienced in his past. He does not realize that he is keeping himself in his own prison. If he does not let go of the past and make a change in the way he thinks, he is headed toward certain destruction. There is still hope for this man and perhaps he will choose to make the necessary changes before it is too late.

Perhaps you can relate to this story. It is never too late for anyone to change their mind. There is hope and there is help. We have been created by a God of love and His desire is to give us all things good. God is always giving, God never takes from us. He only gives us what we choose to receive. If we choose to receive things that are harmful to us then God is the power inside us that makes this happens. If we choose to receive things that are beneficial to us and things that improve our lives then God is the power inside us that makes this happen. God does not ever choose for us. We have been given a free will to choose any way we want to be. God is the giver of life and is the power and energy that makes any and all things exist and operate. God gives life to our thoughts and causes our thoughts to become our reality. We choose our thoughts and we choose our reality. We must really understand this before we can make any lasting change. We must take personal responsibility for our own way of thinking now no matter what our past has been. God never will choose anything for us but God is always there to help us. If we never ask for God's help in changing our mental state then we will not be very successful in making a change. When we ask for God's help He will give us as much as we will receive. When we are receiving from God we are walking in faith. We must be honest with God, which is really being honest with ourselves because God already knows everything there is to know. If you have a problem in your way of thinking, such as anger, blaming, doubt, resentment, fear, or anything else that is having a negative and harmful result in your life then ask God to help you change your way of thinking. Psalms 51: 10 – 12: "Create in me a clean heart, O God and renew a right spirit within me. Cast me not away from thy presence and take not thy Holy Spirit from me. Restore unto me the joy of thy salvation and uphold me with thy free spirit." We can do nothing on our own but we can do anything we desire with God's help.

Philippians 4:13 "I can do all things through Christ which strengthened me." Christ is not a person but is the power of God which resides inside each one of us. God wants us to depend on His power to guide and fulfill our lives. We have nothing to lose but pain and suffering and everything good to gain when we rely on the power of God to live out our lives. Emmet Fox said, "The door to our soul opens inward." When we make contact with God we always do it inwardly. God is in us. He is not a person or entity outside somewhere. The power we need and want is waiting right within us always ready to go to work to give us whatever we desire. Our desires are our thoughts. If we are thinking in a negative way these kinds of thoughts will be brought forth in our lives. Change your thoughts with God's help and you change your life. You can and will experience true peace and happiness if you do this.

Become willing to change

Forgive everyone who has harmed you
Let go of the past – replace it with now.
May you become the master of your own thought life.

About the Author

Founder of TSO Network Youth Theatre Church, Founder of Teens Speaking Out Radio Show and Performing Art Theatre Group, Founder of No More Pain Radio Show, Founder of the North East Mississippi Performing Arts Playhouse, Founder of Operation Hope Educational and Developmental Corporation, Pastor, Motivational Speaker, Counsellor, Life Coach, Teacher and Mentor. He lives in Albany, Georgia, with his wife.

David Hatch is the writer of the books, "Teens Speaking Out Are You Listening?", writer of the gospel musical plays: "The Will To Survive, I've Got It!" – based on his homeless episode and the people he met while homeless; "I Gotta Make A Change", "What About The Children Now?" and "A March Toward The Promise Land".

David has a Ph.D. in Christian Psychology, Master in Theology, and B.A. in Biblical Studies from Jacksonville Theological Seminary, three years in Business Administration, Mississippi Valley State University and two years in Computer Science, Waubonsee College.

"No More Pain" is of utmost important to David because domestic violence and sexual abuse directly affected his family. This personal experience awakened a great desire for him to something about it and he couldn't rest until he did. Through this book David wants to help people expose their perpetrators and seek spiritual and professional help for themselves.

26998316R00048

Made in the USA
Charleston, SC
26 February 2014